ALL STRANGE AWAY

From the same publishers

Samuel Beckett

Novels

Dream of Fair to Middling Women (1932)
Murphy (1938)
Watt (1945)
First Love (1945)
Mercier and Camier (1946)
Molloy (1951)*
Malone Dies (1951)*

The Unnamable (1953) *
How It Is (1961)
Company (1980)**
Ill Seen Ill Said (1981)**
Worstward Ho (1983)**
* published together as the Trilogy
** published together as Nohow On

Short Prose

More Pricks than Kicks (1934)
Collected Short Prose (in preparation)
Beckett Shorts (see below)

Poetry

Collected Poems (1930-1978)
Anthology of Mexican Poetry
(translations)

Criticism
Proust & Three Dialogues with Georges Duthuit (1931,1949)
Disjecta (1929-1967)

Beckett Shorts (A collection of 12 short volumes to commemorate the writer's death in 1989)

1. Texts for Nothing (1947-52)
2. Dramatic Works and Dialogues (1938-67)
3. All Strange Away (1963)
4.Worstward Ho (1983)
5. Six Residua (1957-72)
6. For to End Yet Again (1960-75)

7. The Old Tune (1962)
8. First Love (1945)
9. As the Story Was Told
10. Three Novellas (1945-6)
11. Stirrings Still (1986-9)
12. Selected Poems (1930-85)

ALL STRANGE AWAY

Samuel Beckett

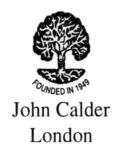

John Calder
London

This edition first published 1999 in Great Britain by
John Calder Publishers
London

Originally published by Gotham Book Mart with illustrations by
Edward Gorey 1976, subsequently in the Journal of Beckett Studies
1978, and then by John Calder (Publishers) Ltd. 1978, 1979

ISBN 0 7145 38582
Paperback

British Library Cataloguing in Publication Data
A catalogue record for this title is available from the British
Library

Printed in Canada by Webcom Ltd

ALL STRANGE AWAY

IMAGINATION dead imagine. A place, that again. Never another question. A place, then someone in it, that again. Crawl out of the frowsy deathbed and drag it to a place to die in. Out of the door and down the road in the old hat and coat like after the war, no, not that again. Five foot square, six high, no way in, none out, try for him there. Stool, bare walls when the light comes on, women's faces on the walls when the light comes on. In a corner when the light comes on tattered syntaxes of Jolly and Draeger Praeger Draeger, all right. Light off and let him be, on the stool, talking to himself in the last person, murmuring, no sound, Now where is he, no, Now he is here. Sitting, standing, walking, kneeling, crawling, lying, creeping, in the dark and in the light, try all. Imagine light. Imagine light. No visible source, glare at full, spread all over, no shadow, all six planes shining the same, slow on, ten seconds on earth to full, same off, try that. Still his crown touches the ceiling, moving not, say a lifetime of walking bowed and full height when brought to a stand. It goes out, no matter, start again, another place, someone in it, keep glaring, never see, never find, no end, no matter. He says, no sound, The longer he lives and so the further goes the smaller they grow, the reasoning being the fuller he fills the space and so on, and the emptier, same reasoning. Hell this light from nothing no reason any moment, take off his coat, no, naked, all right, leave it for the moment. Sheets of black paper, stick them to the wall with cobweb and spittle, no good, shine like the rest. Imagine what needed, no more, any given moment, needed no more, gone, never was. Light flows, eyes close, stay closed till it ebbs, no, can't do that, eyes stay open, all right, look at that later. Black bag over his head, no good, all the rest still in light, front, sides, back, between the legs. Black shroud, start search for pins. Light on, down on knees, sights pin, makes for it, light out, gets pin

9

in dark, light on, sights another, light out, so on, years of time on earth. Back on the stool in the shroud saying, That's better, now he's better, and so sits and never stirs, clutching it to him where it gapes, till it all perishes and rots off of him and hangs off of him in black flitters. Light out, long dark, candle and matches, imagine them, strike one to light, light on, blow out, light out, strike another, light on, so on. Light out, strike one to light, light on, light all the same, candlelight in light, blow out, light out, so on. No candle, no matches, no need, never were. As he was, in the dark any length, then the light when it flows till it ebbs any length, then again, so on, sitting, standing, walking, kneeling, crawling, lying,

10

creeping, all any length, no paper, no pins, no candle, no matches, never were, talking to himself no sound in the last person any length, five foot square, six high, all white when light at full, no way in, none out. Falling on his knees in the dark to murmur, no sound, Fancy is his only hope. Surprised by light in this posture, hope and fancy on his lips, crawling lifelong habit to a corner here shadowless and similarly sinking head to ground shining back into his eyes. Imagine eyes burnt ashen blue and lashes gone, lifetime of unseeing glaring, jammed open, one lightning wince per minute on earth, try that. Have him say, no sound, No way in, none out, he's not here. Tighten it round him, three foot square, five

high, no stool, no sitting, no kneeling, no lying, just room to stand
and revolve, light as before, faces
as before, syntaxes upended in op-
posite corners. The back of his
head touches the ceiling, say a lifetime of standing bowed. Call floor
angles deasil a, b, c and d and
ceiling likewise e, f, g and h, say
Jolly at b and Draeger at d, lean
him for rest with feet at a and head
at g, in dark and light, eyes glaring,
murmuring, He's not here, no
sound, Fancy is his only hope.
Physique, flesh and fell, nail him
to that while still tender, nothing
clear, place again. Light as before,
all white still when at full, flaking
plaster or the like, floor like
bleached dirt, aha. Faces now
naked bodies, eye level, two per

12

wall, eight in all, all right, details later. All six planes hot when shining, aha. So dark and cold any length, shivering more or less, feeble slaps want of room at all flesh within reach, little stamps of hampered feet, so on. Same system light and heat with sweat more or less, cringing away from walls, burning soles, now one, now the other. Murmur unaffected, He's not here, no sound, Fancy dead, gaping eyes unaffected. See how light stops at five soft and mild for bodies, eight no more, one per wall, four in all, say all of Emma. First face alone, lovely beyond words, leave it at that, then deasil breasts alone, then thighs and cunt alone, then arse and hole alone, all lovely beyond words. See how he crouches down and back to see, back of head against face when eyes on cunt, against breasts when on hole, and vice versa, all most clear. So in this soft and mild, crouched down and back with hands on knees to hold himself together, say deasil first from face through hole then back through face, murmuring, imagine him kissing, caressing, licking, sucking, fucking and buggering all this stuff, no sound. Then halt and up to position of rest, back of head touching the ceiling, gaze on ground, lifetime of unbloody bowed unseeing glaring. Imagine lifetime, gems, evenings with Emma and the flights by night, no not that again. Physique, too soon, perhaps never, vague bowed body bonewhite when light at full, nothing clear but

14

ashen glare as imagined, no, attitudes too with play of joints most clear more various now. For nine and nine eighteen that is four feet and more across in which to kneel, arse on heels, hands on thighs, trunk best bowed and crown on ground. And even sit, knees drawn up, trunk best bowed, head between knees, arms round knees to hold all together. And even lie, arse to knees diagonal ac, feet say at d, head on left cheek at b. Price to pay and highest lying more flesh touching glowing ground. But say not glowing enough to burn and turning over, see how that works. Arse to knees, say bd, feet say at c, head on right cheek at a. Then arse to knees say again ac, but feet at b and head on left cheek at d. Then

15

arse to knees say again bd, but feet at a and head on right cheek at c. So on other four possibilities when begin again. All that most clear. Imaginable too flat on back, knees drawn up, hands holding shins to hold all together, glare on ceiling, whereas flat on face by no stretch. Place then most clear so far but of him nothing and perhaps never save jointed segments variously disposed white when light at full. And always there among them somewhere the glaring eyes now clearer still in that flashes of vision few and far now rive their unsee-ingness. So for example as chance may have it on the ceiling a fly-speck or the insect itself or a strand of Emma's motte. Then lost and all the remaining field for

16

hours of time on earth. Imagination dead imagine to lodge a second in that glare a dying common house or dying window fly, then fall the five feet to the dust and die or die and fall. No, no image, no fly here, no life or dying here but his, a speck of dirt. Or hers since sex not seen so far, say Emma standing, turning, sitting, kneeling, lying, in dark and light, saying to herself, She's not here, no sound, Fancy is her only hope, and Emmo on the walls, first the face, handsome beyond words, then deasil details later. And how crouching down and back she turns murmuring, Fancy her being all kissed, licked, sucked, fucked and so on by all that, no sound, hands on knees to hold herself together. Till halt and up, no, no image, down, for her down, to sit or kneel, kneel, arse on heels, hands on thighs, trunk bowed, breasts hanging, crown on ground, eyes glaring, no, no image, eyes closed, long lashes black when light, no more glare, never was, long black hair strewn when light, murmuring, no sound, Fancy dead. Any length, in dark and light, then topple left, arse to knees say db, feet say at c, head on left cheek at a, left breast puckered in the dust, hands, imagine hands. Imagine hands. Let her lie so from now on, have always lain so, head on left cheek in black hair at a and the rest the only way, never sat, never knelt, never stood, no Emmo, no need, never was. Imagine hands. Left on ball of right shoulder holding enough not to slip, right lightly clenched on ground, something in this hand, imagine later, something soft, clench tight, then lax and still any length, then tight again, so on, imagine later. Highest point from ground top of swell of right haunch, say twenty inches, slim woman. Ceiling wrong now, down two foot, perfect cube now, three foot every way, always was, light as before, all bonewhite when at full as before, floor like bleached dirt, something there, leave it for the moment. Waste height, sixteen inches, strange, say some reason unimaginable now, imagine later, imagination dead imagine all strange away. Jolly and Draeger gone, never were. So far then hollow cube three foot overall, no

19

way in imagined yet, none out. Black cold any length, then light slow up to full glare say ten seconds still and hot glare any length all ivory white all six planes no shadow, then down through deepening greys and gone, so on. Walls and ceiling flaking plaster or suchlike, floor like bleached dirt, aha, something there, leave it for the moment. Call floor angles deasil a, b, c and d and in here Emma lying on her left side, arse to knees along diagonal db with arse toward d and knees towards b through neither at either because too short and waste space here too some reason yet to be imagined. On left side then arse to knees db and consequently arse to crown along wall da though not flush because arse out with head on left cheek at a and remaining segment knees to feet along bc not flush because knees out with feet at c. In dark and light. Slow fade of ivory flesh when ebb ten seconds and gone. Long black hair when light strewn over face and adjacent floor. Uncover right eye and cheekbone vivid white for long black lashes when light. Say again though no real image puckered tip of left breast, leave right a mere name. Left hand clinging to right shoulder ball, right more faint loose fist on ground till fingers tighten as though to squeeze, imagine later, then loose again and still any length, so on. Murmuring, no sound, though say lips move with faint stir of hair, whether none emitted or air too rare, Fancy is her only hope, or, She's not here, or, Fancy dead, suggesting moments of discouragement, imagine other murmurs. In dark and light, no, dark alone, say murmurs now in dark alone as though in light all ears all six planes all ears when shining whereas in dark unheard, this a well-known thing. And yet no sound, well say a sound too faint for mortal ear. Imagine other murmurs. So great need of words not daring till at last slow ebb ten seconds, too fast, thirty now, great need not daring till at last slow ebb thirty seconds on earth through a thousand darkening greys till out and incontinent, Fancy dead, for instance if spirits low, no sound. But see how the light dies down

and from half down or more slow
up again to full and the words
down again that were trembling
up, all right, say mere delay, dark
must be in the end, say dark and
light here equal in the end that is
when all done with dead imagining
and measures taken dark and light
seen equal in the end. And indeed
how stay of flow or ebb at any grey
any length and even on the very
sill of black any length till at last
in and black and at long last the
murmur too faint for mortal ear.
But murmurs in long dark so long
that longing no but need for light
as in long light for dark murmurs
sometimes as great a space apart
as from on earth a winter to a
summer day and coming on that
great silence, She's not here, for

instance if in better spirits or, Fancy is her only hope, too faint for mortal ear. And other times to imagine other extreme so hard on one another any order and sometimes when all spent if not assuaged a second time in some quite different so run together that a mere torrent of hope and unhope mingled and submission amounting to nothing, get all this clearer later. Imagine other murmurs, Mother mother, Mother in heaven, Mother of God, God in heaven, combinations with Christ and Jesus, other proper names in great numbers say of loved ones for the most part and cherished haunts, imagine as needed, unsupported interjections, ancient Greek philosophers ejaculated with place of

origin when possible suggesting
pursuit of knowledge at some
period, completed propositions
such as, She is not here, the excep-
tion, imagine others, This is not
possible, there is one, and here
another of exceptional length, In a
hammock in the sun and here the
name of some bewitching site she
lies sleeping. But sudden gleam
that whatever words given to let
fall soundless in the dark that if no
sound better none, all right, try
sound and if no better say quite
speechless, imagine sound and not
till then all that black hair toss
back into the corner baring face as
about to when this happened.
Quite audible then now for her and
if other ears there with her in the
dark for them and if ears low down

in the wall at a for them a voice
without meaning, hear that. Then
further quite expressionless, ohs
and ahs copulate cold and no more
feeling apparently in hammock
than in Jesus Christ Almighty.
And finally for the moment and
then that face the tailaway so
common in untrained speakers
leaving sometimes in some doubt
such things as which Diogenes and
what fancy her only. Such then the
sound roughly and if no clearer so
then all the storm unspoken and
the silence unbroken unless sound
of light and dark or at the moments
of change a sound of flow thirty
seconds till full then silence any
length till sound of ebb thirty seconds till black then silence any
length, that might repay hearing

and she hearing open then her eyes
to lightening or darkening greys
and not close them then to keep
them closed till next sound of
change till full light or dark, that
might well be imagined. But at the
same time say here all sound most
doubtful though still too soon to
deny and that in the end that is
when all gone from mind and all
mind gone that then none ever
been but only silent flesh unless
with the faint rise and fall of breast
the breath to whip up to a pant if
too faint alone and all others
denied but still too soon. Hollow
cube then three foot overall, full
glare, head on left cheek in angle a
and the rest the only way and say
though no clear image now the
long black hair now scattered clear

27

of face on floor so clear when strewn on face now gone some reason, come back to that later, and on the face now bare all the glare for the moment. Gone the remembered long black lashes vivid white so clear before through gap in hair before all tossed back and lost some reason and face quite bare suggesting perhaps confusion then with errant threads of hair itself confused then with long lashes and so gone with hair or some other reason now quite gone. Cease here from face a space to note how place no longer cube but rotunda three foot diameter eighteen inches high supporting a dome semi-circular in section as in the Pantheon at Rome or certain beehive tombs and consequently

three foot from ground to vertex
that is at its highest point no lower
than before with loss of floor space
in the neighbourhood of two square
feet or six square inches per lost
angle and consequences for recum-
bent readily imaginable and of
cubic an even higher figure, all
right, resume face. But a, b, c and
d now where any pair of right-
angled diameters meet circum-
ference meaning tighter fit for
Emma with loss if folded as before
of nearly one foot from crown to
arse and of more than one from
arse to knees and of nearly one
from knees to feet though she still
might be mathematically speaking
more than seven foot long and
merely a question of refolding in
such a way that if head on left

29

cheek at new a and feet at new c
then arse no longer at new d but
somewhere between it and new c
and knees no longer at new b but
somewhere between it and new a
with segments angled more acutely
that is head almost touching knees
and feet almost touching arse, all
that most clear. Rotunda then
three foot diameter and three from
ground to vertex, full glare, head
on left cheek at a no longer new,
when suddenly clear these dimen-
sions faulty and small woman
scarce five foot fully extended
making rotunda two foot diameter
and two from ground to vertex, full
glare, face on left cheek at a and
long segment that is from crown to
arse now necessarily along diagonal too hastily assigned to middle

with result face on left cheek with crown against wall at a and no longer feet but *arse* against wall at c there being no alternative and knees against wall ab a few inches from face and feet against wall bc a few inches from arse there being no alternatives and in this way the body tripled or trebled up and wedged in the only possible way in one half of the available room leaving the other empty, aha.

Diagram

Arms and hands as before for the moment. Rotunda then two foot across and at its highest two foot high, full glare, face on left cheek at a, long black hair gone, long black lashes on white cheekbone gone, glare from above for features on this bonewhite undoubted face right profile still hungering for missing lashes burning down for commissure of lids at least when like say without hesitation hell gaping they part and the black eye appears, leave now this face for the moment. Glare now on hands most womanly clear and womanly especially right still loosely clenched as before but no longer on ground since corrected pose but now on outer of right knee just where it swells to thigh while left still loosely hitched to right shoulder ball as before. All that most clear. That black eye still yawning before going down to former to see what all this squeezing note how the other slips a little way down slope of upper arm then back up to ball, imagine squeeze again. Loose clench any length then crush down most womanly straining knuckles five seconds then back lax any length, all right, now down while fingers loose and in between tips and palm that tiny chink, full glare all this time. No real image but say like red no grey say like something grey and when again squeeze firm down five seconds say faint hiss then silence then back loose two seconds and say faint pop and so arrive though no true image at small grey punctured rubber ball or small grey ordinary rubber bulb such as on earth attached to bottle of scent or suchlike that when squeezed a jet of scent but here alone. So little by little all strange

away. Avalanche white lava mud
seethe lid over eye permitting re-
turn to face of which finally only
that it could be nothing else, all
right. Thence on to neck in health
by nature blank chunk nearer to
healthy natural neck with even
hint of jugular and cords suggesting perhaps past her best and
thence on down to other meat when
suddenly when least expected all
this prying pointless and enough
for the moment and perhaps for
ever this place so clear now when
light at full and this body hinged
and crooked as only the human
man or woman living or not when
light at full without all this poking
and prying about for cracks holes
and appendages. Rotunda then as
before no change for the moment

in dark and light no visible source spread even no shadow slow on thirty seconds to full same off to black two foot high at highest six and a half round good measure, wall peeling plaster or the like supporting dome semi-circular in section same surface, floor bleached dirt or similar, head wedged against wall at a with blank face on left cheek and the rest the only way that is arse wedged against wall at c and knees wedged against wall ab a few inches from face and feet wedged against wall bc a few inches from arse, puckered tip of left breast no real image but maintain for the moment, left hand most clear and womanly lightly clasping right shoulder ball so lightly that slip from time to time down slope of right upper arm then back up to clasp, right no less on upper outer right knee lightly clasping any length small grey rubber sprayer bulb or grey punctured rubber ball then squeeze five seconds on earth faint hiss relax two seconds and pop or not, black right eye like maintain hell gaping any length then seethe of lid to cover imagine frequency later and motive, left also at same time or not or never imagine later, all contained in one hemicycle leaving other vacant, aha. All that if not yet quite complete quite clear and little change likely unless perhaps to complete unless perhaps somehow light sudden gleam perhaps better fixed and all this flowing and ebbing to full and empty more harm than good and soft white unchanging but leave for the moment as seen from outset and never doubted slow on and off thirty seconds to glare and black any length through slow lightening and darkening greys from nothing for no reason yet imagined. Sleep stirring now some time add now with nightmares unimaginable making waking sweet and lying waking till longing for sleep again with dread of demons, perhaps some glimpse of demons later. Dread then in rotunda now with longing and sweet relief but so faint and weak no more than weak tremors of a hothouse leaf. Memories of past felicity no save one faint with faint ripple of sorrow of a lying side by side, look at this closer later. Imagine turning over with help of hinge of neck to bow head towards breast and so temporarily shorten long segment unwedging crown and arse with play enough to writhe till finally head wedged against wall at a as before but on right cheek and arse against wall at c as before but on right cheek and knees against wall a few inches from face as before but wall ad and feet against wall a few inches from arse as before but wall cd and so all tripled up and wedged as before but on the other side to rest the other and within the other hemicycle leaving the other vacant, aha, all that most clear. Clear further how at some earlier more callow stage this writhe again and again in vain through weakness or natural awkwardness or want of pliancy or want of resolution and how half-way through on back with legs just clear how after some time in the balance thus the fall back to where she lay wedged against a wall at a with blank face on left cheek and arse against wall at c and knees against wall ab and feet against wall bc with left hand clutching lightly right shoulder ball and right on upper outer knee small grey sprayer bulb or grey punctured rubber ball with disappointment naturally tinged perhaps with relief and this again and again till final renouncement with faint sweet relief, faint disappointment will have been here too. Sleep if maintained with cacodemons making waking in light and dark if this

39

maintained faint sweet relief and
the longing for it again and to be
gone again a folly to be resisted
again in vain. No memories of
felicity save with faint ruffle of
sorrow of a lying side by side and of
misfortune none, look closer later.
So in rotunda up to now with disappointment and relief with dread
and longing sorrow all so weak
and faint no more than faint tremors
of a leaf indoors on earth in winter
to survive till spring. Glare back
now where all no light immeasur-
able turmoil no sound black soundless storm of which on earth all
being well say one millionth stilled
to mean and of that as much again
by the more fortunate all being well
vented as only humans can. All
gone now and never been never

40

sitll never voiced all back when never sundered unstillable turmoil no sound, She's not here, Fancy is here only, Mother mother, Mother in heaven and of God, God in heaven, Christ and Jesus all combinations, loved ones and places, philosophers and all mere cries, In a hammock etc, and all such, leaving only for the moment, Fancy dead, try that again with spirant barely parting lips in murmur and faint stir of white dust or not in light and dark if this maintained or dark alone as though ears when shining and dead uncertain in dying fall of amateur soliloquy when not known for certain. Last look oh not farewell but last for now on left side tripled up and wedged in half the room head

41

against the wall at a and arse
against wall at c and knees against
wall ab an inch or so from head and
feet against wall bc an inch or so
from arse. Then look away then
back for left hand clasping lightly
right shoulder ball any length till
slip and back to clasp and right on
upper outer knee any length grey
sprayer bulb or small grey punctured rubber ball till squeeze with
hiss and loose again with pop or
not. Long black hair and lashes
gone and puckered breast no
details to add to these for the
moment save normal neck with
hint of cords and jugular and black
bottomless eye. Within apart from
fancy dead and with faint sorrow
faint memory of a lying side by side
and in sleep demons not yet

42

imagined all dark unappeasable
turmoil no sound and so exhaled
only for the moment with faint
sound, Fancy dead, to which now
add for old mind's sake sorrow
vented in simple sighing sound
black vowel a and further so that
henceforth here no other sounds
than these say gone now and never
were sprayer bulb or punctured
rubber ball and nothing ever in
that hand lightly closed on nothing
any length till for no reason yet
imagined fingers tighten then relax
no sound and to the same end slip
of left hand down slope of right
upper arm no sound and same pur-
pose none of breath to the end that
here henceforth no other sounds
than these and never were that is
than sop to mind faint sighing

43

sound for tremor of sorrow at faint
memory of a lying side by side and
fancy murmured dead.